MEDICAL AID

and other poems

Medical Aid and Other Poems

Donald Jones

UNIVERSITY OF NEBRASKA PRESS · Lincoln

Thanks are due the following magazines in which some of these poems first appeared: *Channels, Gallery, little review of the pacific northwest, Massachusetts Review, Penny Poems from Midwestern University, Poet and Critic, Prairie Schooner, Scrip, South Dakota Review, Southern Poetry Review,* and *Steppenwolf.* Thanks are also due the anthology in which "November 22, 1963" first appeared: *Of Poetry and Power: Poems Occasioned by the Presidency and by the Death of John F. Kennedy* (New York: Basic Books, 1964).

For KARL SHAPIRO,

   beneficent where

   "the sky settles all questions"

FOREWORD

Each of the *Medical Aid* poems arose from the claims of a
real welfare client for cold cash, health, and human dignity;
but each case may mislead the maker of generalizations if
he does not play all the poems off against each other.
Though the names of the clients are changed, the facts given
are strictly accurate. The poems owe a special debt to
Wordsworth's blind beggar amid the London crowds and
to Baudelaire's "Les Sept Vieillards."

The *Other Poems* were written over a span of eight
years, willy-nilly compelled by their subjects amid the
variety and incongruity of living in the haunts of America.
My verse lately seems turning toward the West, the plain
talltale, and the sacred-profane, as in "Wild West Christmas," a story after a friend's recurring nightmare.

DONALD JONES

CONTENTS

MEDICAL AID

for Margaret Graham
of Baltimore

PREFACE

Sick of the claims of art,
myopic from close readings,
and rattled by apparatus
for breaking down the Text,

I left my place as fellow
and needing money came
to Medical Aid for a slice
of life and public funds.

Mostly a clerk to check
and ease the flow of help
to illness down under the level
of Minimal Subsistence,

I found on my hand and heart
the duplicate callous growing
of a cynical old pro,
my future closing down.

Turning again to school,
I was amazed one night
when Joseph Sicovsky arose
and made his place a poem.

I couldn't stop his stumbling,
and after, followed the clients
whose ghosts were unappeased
and wreaked their claims on art:

I A PLACE FOR JOSEPH SICOVSKY

From the filth on the harbor's edge
rose Joseph Sicovsky, stumbling
to the State for Medical Aid
to Aged shambles of legs.

He made his claim in the stupor
of years of bedless rest
and slept, head hung, at my desk
as I dialed my way through his past.

Aside from the brown paper bag
he had with him, his goods were locked
in a rusted chest at his daughter's
but someone had stolen the key

some night when he slept, as usual,
in a truck that was parked unlocked
or lightly on marble steps
but never in his daughter's home.

A burden to no one person,
he lived on his verified income
of forty-five dollars a month,
his Veterans' Compensation.

Clearly, the State could help—
but when to a routine query
he dumbly took from his pocket
his grime-edged pack of credentials

and showed me his mortgage-book,
thirteen dollars a month
paid without fail on his house,
vacant, the windows all broken—

why, then, the case was altered
and closed to the vagrant landlord;
for the State would not exempt
a house that was not a home.

I turned him away to stumble
sixty blocks out to the City
of Baltimore Public Hospitals,
where fees were said to be nominal.

I heard he had managed to reach it
some six months later, was now
being scrubbed with surgical brushes
all over, before diagnosis.

His payments were punctual still
on his empty real estate,
but someone had stolen the furnace,
the door, and the kitchen-sink.

Stripped naked, scrubbed raw, half asleep,
he must have lain on the table
warm in the thought of the mansions
that lay open in his *own* house.

Bedridden, your wife afraid
of elevators, you'd phoned in
for an official home-visit
to get your medicine free.

Leaving our modern office
and driving the short distance
to the sagging row on Boone Street,
I pulled up nervous and parked.

The black glares of street arabs
and mill-hands out of work
followed me up the steps
of cheap marble to the door.

Wary of bill-collectors,
your wife wouldn't let me in
till I'd given sufficient proofs
of my beneficent mission.

She led me through the parlor,
musty with floral patterns
that faded all over the walls,
the sofa, and torn carpet

to the narrow upstairs bedroom
where wide awake you lay
limbs twisted with pain,
your hair a frame of white.

Supine, you stated your claim
as if upon a platform
with the world for audience
and the Good Lord looking down.

Though I had no reason to doubt
your just entitlement,
I had to have some proof
of income, age, and assets.

I felt rebuked like a child
when your wife brought in a Bible
and you pointed a stiff finger
at your birthdate—"Born in Freedom."

But your one asset, a policy
with the Bad Risk Burial people,
some ninety dollars at death
for a nickel a week paid still

these seventy years you told me,
you wouldn't let me see
for fear the State would take it
and leave you to be dissected.

Nothing I said could convince you
that insurance was safe from us;
and bound by regulations
that cut down fraud and good faith,

I left you to die assured
of rest for your bones, still paying
for the dozens of dear pill-bottles
you'd shown me to prove your claim.

III AS BEST SHE COULD

Old widow crazed with hunger, you came in crippled,
your backcountry eyes bright and furtive, your voice
careening between a whimper and wild thin laughter.

I saw you take the edge of the chair and cower
as the social worker cut through your explanations,
your patches of self-respect, with her curt queries.

Terrible your smile when asked about your holdings
in bonds, in bank accounts, in property,
your look when reminded of life insurance lapsed.

She wouldn't believe you lived as best you could
on the meager uncertain amount your daughters sent you
and paid no rent to an old and kindly landlord.

She took your naked terror of death for greed
and probable fraud, denied you, sent you off
for written proofs from daughters out of state.

Their misspelt notes came in some three weeks later,
your card for medical care went out, but soon
came back from Public Health a cancellation.

No blame attached, the regulations followed,
your death quite likely in any case, but still
I see you rise and quiver away, your stiff heart
pounding with baffled rage, with stifled pride.

IV V. D. PUFFENBURGER

Thick-headed and domineering
with bright-veined eyes and nose,
you cussed me out but good

when I stated that your income,
a Government pension assured,
exceeded the annual limit;

for you'd blown your check this month
(no matter how—we agreed)
and needed medicine now—

a point you emphasized
with your blunt and scaling finger
as rotting you shook with fear.

V REFERRAL FROM OB. PREADMISSION

You sat there a huge lump
with cliché shifty eyes,
applying for State money
to have another kid on.

You showed me your husband's card
to prove his unemployment
and said you didn't know when
or where he might get work.

When I asked what work he did,
you shyly smiled and said
he drove a bulldozer
and was a fine big man.

When I asked you where he'd worked,
you said you didn't remember,
so I asked if he was home now
and called him then and there.

Bright and straightforward, he said
he'd made five bucks an hour
some eight months out of the year
for the past three years or so

and he had his job assured
with the same old outfit
and didn't want help—then added,
you'd catch hell when you got home.

VI PROOF AND REPROOF

Stalwart old gentleman,
a member of grand juries,
you asked if I wanted an oath
from you and raised your hand

Though embarrassed and overawed
I said it wouldn't do,
and you damn near swore and left
but could not afford such pride.

VII CONSIDER THE LILIES

Strong black man of thirty,
a yard- and errand-boy,
you were sitting, you said,
minding your business and beer

when some guy—you don't know who
and the others if they know won't tell—
comes into the bar behind you
and lays you out with a bottle

to the tune of a grand and a half
in intricate silvery pains
of world-famous surgeons and weeks
under square-meal observation.

An apparent modern miracle,
you sat smiling, O.K.,
as I verified the State
would have to foot the bill—

for you had no wages above
the subsistence level for one
and walked out innocent
and free, for all I knew,

to drink the health paid up
by your worried buddies, then sleep
at your Old-Age pensioned mother's,
and take no thought for your life.

VIII   THE WARD SHE LAY IN

Some goddess convalescent,
she lay in a Hollywood pose
on a cramped ward-bed, endowed
with beauty and nineteen years.

Her husband recently drafted,
her baby abandoned to in-laws,
her things in a room she'd stayed in
with a girl-friend since moved out,

she just didn't give a damn,
it seemed, as I smoked and asked
for verifications of how
in the hell she'd managed to live.

Vague and evasive her answers
as her look paused idle and candid,
somewhat amused to have
a visitor take in her charms.

I cleared my throat and out
at the intake office I learned
of her gonorrhea, confirmed
support by means invisible,

and to keep old Mercy solvent,
let the State pick up the tab,
remembering with a twitch
she'd signed her claim with my pen.

Fragile, brunette, well-spoken,
single and over thirty,
her family still in Norway,
she'd bravely come to our country.

Broken by heavy lifting
for the struggling Good-Will people,
mended for a small fortune,
and starving in convalescence,

she walked three miles from the slums
where her rent was overdue,
and wearing the last pretty dress
that hadn't been pawned for food,

she arrived at Medical Aid
to sit down timid and giddy
with her neatly ordered bills
and proofs of her sure goodness.

She spoke of her far country,
its green and simple ways,
her amazement in the toils
of medicine still unsocial.

Feeling we all ahd failed her,
I approved her application
(really quite clear and routine),
then made myself obnoxious

to force for her an early
Emergency Appointment
for General Public Assistance
some seven or eight days later

[14]

and broke the rules to give her
some private cold hard help
including cab-fare back
to the shoreline's wretched refuge.

X TWO JOBS, SO A LATE HOUR

That bedridden blindman who spoke
no word of English, cared for
by his self-effacing son,

on that visit after work
greeted me with strange joy
as if I were the sun—

the torch of America come
to help him through the dark.

But I was the pencil-pusher
who helped him make his mark.

XI CLIENTS AND ROBBERS

Pleasant old colored couple,
living on Social Security
but victims to druggists' charges,
you applied for a little relief.

Your income was slightly over
the low subsistence limit,
but we certified you still
by subtracting sky-high interest—

for to raise a rowhouse breeze
and help your cases of asthma,
you'd signed for a window fan
at nearly triple its worth.

A bad precedent, no doubt,
but poorly schooled and trusting,
you needed some fresh-air loophole
in the clauses of *laissez-faire*.

XII SPECIAL CARE SOMEWHERE

Old man with a mad cackle
drooling all over his bib
as he attacked his oatmeal,

incontinent blank spinstress
for years waiting on her back
with bedsores for the best opiate,

gnarled mother in her own rocker
knocking against her allotted
cramped cube of ward space,

quick seamstress left stranded
by her children, turning out toys
that the director patted her over,

toys that made a flat flapper
so shrill and vicious that the keeper
had to appease her with gross flirting

crazed delicate white hands
arthritically clutched on nothing,
stuck out proudly for pity,

dumb queries shot at the stranger,
malign stares, or smiles and nods
of the helpless prostrate to please—

the almighty's German Shepherd
as I left still growled at me,
helping me think I didn't belong.

XIII AN OLD MAN'S LARK

From the fine nursing home
unnoticed one afternoon
with saved-up spending money
from his children far away

he bolted across the lawn,
caught a streetcar downtown,
had two cheeseburgers, a malt,
and watched a double feature.

His money all gone, he spent
the summer night on a park bench,
was found there the next morning
by his helpers young and hurt.

XIV A SPECIAL CASE

Rather well tailored and groomed,
balding and pressed for time,
you came wincing at the others
for Medical Aid to your mother.

You were at pains to make clear
that you could richly cover
her failing health's expenses
and would prefer to do so,

but that proud like all the aged,
she would not be a burden,
if she could help it, on any
of her many willing children.

Already late for a conference,
you left me a number for calling
your secretary in private
on the progress of this matter.

Your mother was duly entitled,
and having called the number,
I saw your wife, who dropped by
for the card, well dressed and haggard.

Though I never saw your mother,
I saw *you* once more; but avoiding
my eye, you wouldn't help me
as you clerked in Shirts at Christmas.

XV MRS. STANDISH

She had a chic cloche,
that stiff-necked Negress
who wouldn't scrub our linoleum.

I thought she'd work out all right,
that light-brown client,
husband dying of cancer

but determined to pay
more than they could and let me let
the State do the rest.

I saw swank notes that proved
the usual rate for day's work
with irrelevant praises

and thought I'd help her
with no risk and have a steady
chore-girl (the old snob!)

to clean up after us
and take the money to help
keep her on her feet.

But she'd just polish the silver,
dust, and handwash your nylons,
so we canned her.

XVI MRS. STATTON

Come to recertify
her claim for free care,
I tripped on the stairs.

Her bell didn't work,
the hall stank and was dark,
and I knocked and knocked.

At last with curses
at the scraping door, she peered
from her third-floor perch.

Reassured
that I wasn't a thug or a drunk,
she backed by the sink

to let me in
through the kitchen squalor
to the junk-littered parlor.

With dignity
she asked that I be seated
in a rickety rocker that squeaked.

The light better,
I saw her clean shrewd face,
her stained and ancient dress.

The proud child
of pillars of the old city,
she now was starving and eighty,

at pains to impress
on my probably scoffing mind
the fact she'd had a maid,

her father a carriage,
her long-dead husband a practice
of prominent patients.

Left broken
by his and their son's protracted,
fatal, and ruinous sickness,

she'd worked,
till too old, as a common clerk
for her fifty-dollar Security,

her body
willed to Johns Hopkins but free
from any nurse's liberty.

She claimed
to have a doctor's degree
from an Ivy League University,

seemed alarmed
when I mentioned my master's
to help the visit pleasantly pass,

and fled to *Time,*
the copies given her that kept
her mind from "preying on itself,"

then screeched out
a popular song she'd published, adept
in thinking up rhymes while she slept.

With apologies
she served me a glass of water
on a clean refolded napkin and saucer,

and as I left,
promising to come back and talk
about old Poe and her novel safely locked,

she had me pry open
her kitchen window that a storm
had stuck shut, perhaps to keep her from harm.

XVII CROSSWAYS

A world-travelled Veteran sailor
but now in tow to Johns Hopkins,
you roomed with fellow gypsies
and wandered Broadway Market.

Your intestines had been rerouted
with some success, but you'd keep
knocking about till rupture
brought you back to Emergency.

Your pension a bit in excess,
I'd proved with close detail
the Extraordinary Expenses
of your vital apparatus,

and to stop the duplication
of your circuitous case
and save State money, I'd asked
that you always ask for me.

> So again, as you calmly told over
> your latest admission, the distance
> you'd passed by death—I reviewed,
> renewed your old entitlement.

And then those few minutes past,
we drew out the ceremony
as was only fitting, and talked
about our crossing ways.

Serene and weather-beaten,
your hair turned yellowish-grey,
at your neck a ragged bandana
of checkered rust, you talked

about the unchanging tides,
the world-moving moon at full,
and, laughing, told my fortune
with perfect ease and candor.

Buzzed that another was waiting,
I shook your hand and wished you
a run of good luck, but hoping
somehow for another rupture.

XVIII COMPOSITE

The former highsteel worker
lay flat on a bed in the ward
complaining that someone had stolen
the glass eye he'd left in a pan.

My visit was quite uncalled-for:
already on Public Assistance,
his case was a clear-cut Active
Hospital Certification.

I told the charity worker
about his missing part;
not alarmed, she said it would be
replaced in the overhead.

Back again a week later,
I learned he'd died soon after
as rolled from the surgeon's hand
he'd lost his balance and lost.

The intake worker was shocked
when I asked who'd come to claim him,
and she called at once to discover
that the patient was waiting still.

She said that steps would be taken,
but I didn't follow him up
to the room where students broke down
his skill in structural building.

OTHER POEMS

NEWSBOY: LARAMIE, WYOMING

The news was fresh and hot
    that nine years old,
wrapped like a mummy, I brought
    through the spell of cold.

And the charm of matter-of-fact
    would open a door
to thaw me, zero-attacked
    in the new Cold War.

THE BLIZZARD OF '49
For Wm. C. Wms.

Zing! went the skier
blue cap
yellow sweater
chrome skis

a chunk of lead
down the
shovelled-up
snow bank!

GREEK BELLY-DANCER AT THE
BROADWAY ACROPOLIS

The mood embodied flows
and backward bends
before the crowd—who knows
where the body ends?

HONOR-BRIGHT

You loved me just
for fun. In trust
you let me home
but could not come

with one so crossed
he dreaded lust,
played keeps, and lost.
You loved me just.

LABYRINTH

The hard sharp curves
of your legs crossed
sheer on my nerves
make me stand lost

in a maze of thread
where you'd have me led
not naked to bed
but dead in your stead.

ORPHIC WRONG

Your great clear eyes
and elegant thighs
tear me apart—
here, have a heart!

Surprised? Hell no!
You knew how I'd go
if you'd just play
at looking that way.

ON FIRST LOOKING INTO DR. BERNE'S
GAMES PEOPLE PLAY

The drunk who gets
his payoff in shame,
the dry with debts
who ruins his name,
each plays a game.

The flirt who sets
the mind aflame
of the fop who bets
she's a frigid dame,
both play the same game.

The guest who upsets
his coffee to claim
unconscious regrets
that he ever came,
enjoys his game.

The wife who besets
her husband with blame
for the welcomed threats
that keep her tame,
saves face by her game.

The father who frets
when the boys exclaim
at his own nymphets
who fan his flame,
plays a roaring game.

The hard coquettes
whose lures became
tight courtroom nets
for the men they'd maim,
cry "rape" at their game.

The robber who sweats
lest he miss the fame
of police gazettes
takes careless aim,
and wins his game.

And the patient forgets
why his leg went lame,
an excuse that lets
his Adult disclaim
his sprint in that game.

But as each forgets
how he plays some game
in the dark, and gets
deeper in shame
and grave regrets,

may your book reclaim
each from his game
who reads its comic name
and laughingly disclaims
his freedom from such games.

SING A SONG OF NO CENTS

To the stern police
of Calvinsburg
where fists are tight
and burglars wander

some burgher reported
the crickets who squander
their art on the night,
disturbing the peace.

WINTER OF THE SOCIAL BODY

On any level heartland harvested
against the wailing edge, the unstacked straw
is dealt at random, landless lots are cast.

Upon that table hands with spades in dread
contract unbidden, laws of chance withdraw
the hearts, the shocks, until the spades hold fast.

A SOD HOUSE MEMORIAL

We broke the sod for our bread
    and shared, hoping for birth
against the Arctic edge,
    sown shelter in the earth:
the grave and darkening need
of mother, man, and seed.

Up grew through grace of rain
    and blazing summer sun
the painful harvest home
    where all in praise is done:
our deed brought forth the grain
that filled with sons the plain.

UPLAND GAME

For Pat Callahan

That dawn this dead of winter,
rising before the farmers,
we stalked against the wind
through the spectral covers of earth.

From edges of frost and drouth
the rabbits leapt their lightning,
the quail burst thundering up,
our small hail harried late.

Quick as our breath new silence
fell back within the wind,
the weedstalks quivered still
as our safeties clicked on loud.

Thrashing through grey thickets,
we stopped short at an owl
dusky in gnarled branches
glaring against the sunrise.

That hunter stretched and soared
deep in the youth of the world
while we latecomers stumbled
under his darkening arc.

LAMENT OF TWO OCTOBERS

—"Heavy with brittle bloom
earth-curved sighs grew still

when clothed in profound blue
and gentle grey she stole

within the leaf-laid wood,
glided through the sun's dull lapse,

from a thickening brook wooed
her innocent eyes, then laughed

and called the autumn good."—

AT MRS. ANDERSON'S

Gorgeous in April storm the lilacs flourish
around her sallow-painted house with roof
the shade of rust.

            Her skeleton aerial,
stainless in the thick rain, charms pulsing streams
to flickering shadows white or grey or black
that wink as perching stiff to squint, she rasps
a shrill laugh along the spidered banister
by which her glove-thin hand had pulled her heart,
in throb of August, a step too high.

                    Released
now from the tight mask that bathed her veins
past Winter's ice, she lifts her wilted face
to tell the time, puts out the lifelike shades,
and through her home of unswept caverns gropes
for her appointed pills the color of Spring:
auroral orange, pink, soft violet,
and green.

            Widow hid from swaying green
and winds of sustenance, O may your heart
with color swell and, lilac blown, fly swift
beyond your narrow chambers in the storm
past earth, past imaged pulses, breath, or name.

WREATH FOR GRANDMOTHER

I *When*

Long distance brought her death
    touching us home,
    then left the hum
of a contact broken, deaf.

Wind poured through the black phone,
    the country's weather
    calling together
with her: "The same. Just fine."

II *Then*

Hurtled on a straight track
    Denver Zephyr behind
    the flowers of Western Union
we crash on the gaudy bank
beyond her abysmal home.

III *Now*

The blacktop rolls over
the blackberry patch
trucks squash the beanrows
rusted beercans attack
the strawberry runners
speed-warnings mock
the flat scarecrow
and litter and weeds
choke out the stray seeds
of her earth-turning deeds.

[45]

Now she is gone

bent frail to the edges
of her urban lot
where glads and morning glories
motley of tulips and flares of iris
break out on the ledges
of stucco cement and lawn
and cut will brighten the plot
of the man the garden fed
or dull as recurring stories
wilt by the warm bed

where jets shake the newly dead.

CAEDMON'S HYMN

Now should we carol   the sky-realm's King,
the might of the Maker,   His motive unmoved,
the World-Father's works,   as He wrought every wonder,
Lord Eternal,   in time's dark dawn.
First He fashioned   for children of earth
the sheltering heavens,   O Holy Creator;
the middle kingdom   then mankind's Keeper,
Lord Eternal,   turned to the light
and made it our garden,   O God of all might!

TWO RAVENS
Genesis 8:21

The windows of heaven swung to—
then Noah opened a square
through the dark of his flood-rocked wall
but nowhere saw dry land.

The raven waving to his sad wife
flew out above the waters
but only the ark had rest
and he found nowhere to light.

At dusk on the seventh day
the holy dove came home
bright with a branch of olive
sprung from under ocean.

By then the raven had fallen,
gone thin and far as a shadow,
safe on an apple branch
gnarled as the bird's dry feet.

Warm breezes dried the waters
but he swayed on the limb and waited
for his wife to cross the rainbow
for their feast on man's dark heart.

NOVEMBER 22, 1963

There the guard changes,
the Soldier stays
abstract and stiff
within his tomb.

Here in Nebraska
the wind bursts
over the bare space
of the nation's heart—

our son and father
Known but turned to flame
against the vast affront
we bear time out of mind.

ONE FOR CLAWSON, COHEN, HOLLINGS-HEAD, JONES, MORTON, JOHNSON, KOSYGIN, MAO, ETC.

German and Jewish,
Welsh and Scot,
English and Irish
and Huguenot,

we five on the Fourth
swung in the park
and rose with sky-rockets
alive on the dark.

The bombs bursting in air,
we sang out the strains
of our freedom once won
to the lilt of our chains.

Then with those rainbows
touching dark ground,
we worked together
the merry-go-round.

While bombers sped
their Arctic round,
we dreamed in bed
of common ground.

TALKING ABOUT HELP

"Remember Miss Bessie—
fat, shiny brown
sent to us
by our friends downstairs?"

"Sure, she kept the floor spotless
but she got into things
as when she broke the bottle
of Chanel that you kept
snug in its sniff-proof box."

"She liked us, I think,
seemed tickled
by us whites with no T.V.,
had plenty of room to turn
in our barely furnished place,
and joked to cheer me
when our Kemtone dried
loud gold and pink."

"She winked at me once
over the girdle you'd let dry
on a rack for records
and you had to reassure her
that a hysterectomy
wouldn't lose her her boy-friend."

"Yes, but she worked hard
though she didn't eat much
and among the many
cans of pop you got her
she wouldn't touch the black-cherry."

AN OVERHEARD RHYME IN TIME

You say I'm mad
but ask my dad
who's mad (not sad
or glad) I'm mad.

I join his corps
am mad for war
am glad before
I see the gore.

I rhyme and count
the bodies mount
on his account
of Christ on Mount.

I rhyme to speak
am harmless, meek
turning my cheek
His smile to seek.

You say I'm mad
but ask that Dad
Who's glad and sad
(not mad) I'm mad.

WILD WEST CHRISTMAS

The blizzard rattled the pane

and God walked the corridor
of the firetrap cheap hotel.

Past numbered huddles He strode,
spurs clanging the way clear,
His draw quick and His aim death.

His double threw his shadow
defiantly down from the bright
hard flesh of his talltale youth.

That shadow catching God's eye,
they drew point-blank and fired.

The shadow and God and the glass
shattered to stars of the sky
but the boy and the dark pane fell.

*—And over the wind-bit plain
the wandering gunmen tell
of the brave boy who brought down **God**
to harrow his soul from hell.*

FOR A FORMER INMATE

Why turn this verse to you?
What have you now to do
with any life at all?

The cars that coupled this fall
came bringing express to all
a good for every need.

Your verses, your one deed,
delivered less—recede
before that Westering track

that turns no vision back
to the space of time, the crack
when you stuck out your neck.

What need had you to kneel
there to the bar of steel
and leave not even a wreck?

But what had you then to do
when no straight mind could feel
the hell your head went through?

ANTIPHONIES LAUNCHED BEFORE
For Dale

Coming back nightbound to the rail
on the Staten Island Ferry
where I'd left you with a dark smile,
I dropped the steaming coffee

sudden in terror and stared
down into the tortuous wake
drowning itself cold hours
from the vault of the Bridge that broke

its downward string of light
against the harboring dark
where the Torch and star-topped towers
beaconed but for despair.

No cry, no hand came through
the enormity swept back,
and wordless I then knew
how estranged and lone you were—

but coming up you smiled,
remarked you'd been to the john,
and were surprised as wild
with light I was to the rail drawn.

MANHATTAN

The legend fell to glory
    as surging we travelled
to the loom of the hundreth story
    where our wits unravelled.

NIGHTCLUB

Against the glare of mind's strange work
    the bar again is closed;
    we glow at ease, suppose
all our familiars in near dark.

Through rose-soft lightning ivory rains,
    the cool wind comes and blows
    our sense to the end of blues
where need lies naked arched with pain.

One will, we grope out past the check
    and gather hard and fast
    our rainbow-potted feast
against the glare of mind's strange work.

A VIEW OF BALTIMORE

O Monumental City the bronze turns green
like wreckage under water: Johns Hopkins and Luther
command their corners, the dead rowhouses recede.

Astride their sea-changed horses Robert E. Lee
and Stonewall Jackson gain no ground while across
the lawn vague Victory holds still the Union.

Between the limestone lions that shed the climate,
the Thinker bends, losing himself in the flux
of the elements, his thought knotted with constipation.

In a thicket where hobos sleep the night off, dark Poe
emerges lurid as his strange City in the Sea,
rattle of mockingbird floating through judas flowers.

From his grey baroque erection the Father of Our Country
ejaculates himself and "looks gigantically down."

AN INTERIOR MOSAIC
OF THE BISHOP'S CITY
For Joan

The Bay's waters, in a moment gliding
through the wide mirror, move from sleep
each emerald bank and brilliant building,
swell under the Arc of Crimson Gilding,
and westward blend with blues more deep
as azure of morning melts from their sweep.

To Cal we saunter, rounding the air
to full-breathed catches of slight sense,
and finding the Campanile there,
we buy round trips. The mortared square,
with chimes for tassels, with grave suspense
for Humpty-Dumpties, with its immense

extension course of arts and learning,
squints our pupils to attention
with arched temptations for spurning
the fallen apples and angels burning
in Bishop Berkeley's Genial Sun,
all neighbors to the drab cyclotron.

Hungry, we are put in touch with the ground
not by the wireless but by stout cable;
above, we hear the shattering sound
of the hour's crystal. Not having found
free fruits upon the green-splashed table
checkered with sidewalks, and being able

to pay a leering grocer for two
moist apples torn, some afternoon,
from an eastern valley, we consume

their subtle cells, dense as the bloom
swaddling the brown-husked Church of One,
drowned in the flowing honey of the sun.

The dappled day knelt and was stabled in the ark
of twisted cables strung through smouldering skies;
then all our visions were levelled under an arc
of thickest shadow. I told, in parting, the spark
of radiant spirals above you to protect the wise
dark circles widening in your brown eyes.

A WAKE

After the shots
of Irish whiskey, scotch,
Canadian smooth, and rotgut wine—
bubbles of whim
on the dark free-floating wills
of haggard people eager to be pleased—
after the boatman's song
spinning in black in drift of smoke
its heart-throb rise and fall to rise—
after the lights of eyes
never to burn the same
ever to break the name
they did not know—
we left for smokes—
we veered to verve
of the world's frayed nerve—
its dewtipped bud
and birdcry, burst
of squirrel in flame of tree
and swoop of sky
wherever we looked—
you flickered and stood
on top of a sawed-off stump
more green of coat
more flame of hair
more welling sky
of blue-green eye
more all of is
than May's own queen—
all on our way to the vending machine.

RONSARD'S "A Hélène"

When you are old some evening near the fire,
winding and spinning threads by candlelight
and marvelling as you sing what I now write,
cry then, "So moved my beauty Ronsard's lyre."

Though half asleep from weaving your attire,
your servants each will hearken with delight
and at the tolling of my name unite
to wish you deathless blessing as one choir.

But I shall lie asleep far underground,
phantasmal form with myrtle shadows wound;
while cowering at your hearth beneath Time's knife,

you will regret my love, your fierce disdain.
Believe me now: tomorrow brings but pain—
seize from this day the blossoms of our life.

REST STOP

Showing his friend
how he could shoot,
he nailed a bird
at three hundred feet.

How he could shoot
a mourning dove
on a high, taut wire
perched close to his love.

The mourning dove
at the crack of the shot
dropped in a clump
by the road to rot.

At the crack of the shot
his wife not far
asked what bird
he'd shot from the car.

His wife in the car,
his friend as a third,
he started and said,
"Oh, some small bird."

WITHOUT A RESERVATION

Wahoo! tonight there's rain,
a good hard rain, stray thunder

the streets all sudden rivers,
a rare car splashing

my friends and adopted troubles
all snug or restless at home

there reading a book or under the covers,
maybe just having a good hard cry

my wife away for a week
(having just called with love)

our Irish setter pup
festooning the grocery-bag wastebasket

around the house
         —around the house
there's warmth and light and beer

(three quarts all cold and wet
just brought in from the rain)

five hundred books to read,
loved and lingering debts of letters

self-starting long-delayed
reviews and articles to write

(the sad near-hopeless affairs
of friends and the World just now remote

my faults and sorrows, even the third degree
all falling to clear forgiveness)

I am again
              —Wahoo!
(as north in Nebraska)

tonight there's a good hard rain
and here, just here, I am

happy and drinking and writing
even though this only night

(night of lonely splashes, swirling puddles,
and garrulous eavesdroppers)

I just sit here and write,
"I have no poem to write."

LESLIE DAE LINDOU, PROFESSOR OF ENGLISH

Nor all your Tears . . .

I remember him
lurking, chain-smoking
outside the church
where in seven minutes
he'd play the bass, conduct
the requiem he wrote
for his sister.

I remember
in high school then
the auditorium
dark and the quiet
eloquent voice,
his emerald slides
of England.

Remember
in the immense
cold morning
lecture room for freshmen,
he played Debussy
and delivered
the Decalogue of Auden.

His startling
phone call that forgave
the final, his reading
my verse whenever
I had more ready—
too honest and kind
to offer a comment.

That evening
for all his students
with fire and art and apples
in the ample cabin
his family built,
invisible back
on the boulevard.

Contention
loving and ancient
of master and rebel,
the question
I missed on a summer's
exam on Our Tongue,
putting Arthur for Alfred.

Call back
the books exchanged,
Greek brandy, duffers' games
of chess, the time I lured
his class in the moderns
away with my records
of poets reading.

The time that
sharing his office
with an eminent poet on visit,
he left in courteous haste
when backward, bashful,
I brought in
my poems for judgment.

And that last time
come back to town
I found him
so long gone
in a pitiless dying
there in his simple
home of all civility,

the voice for me most noble
a distant whisper
over the deep lung cancer,
the hands so versatile
all fumbling, dumb,
the good life going
over the last homecoming,

and still the music
of his living moves within me
the way of written words
world-scattered back
to the joyous throngs,
all distant, still,
that walk on stage and hill.

FOR JOEY

That autumn under our willow
*   upon our hometown's height*
we watched the near sky follow
*   the mountains into night.*

We chanted spellbound verses
*   to keep the heavens bright*
as the wind came up with voices
*   that shook against the night.*

The leaves were thrown in thunder
*   upon the storm's far might*
but we kept for shelter under
*   our tree that branched in night*

and felt our art's endurance
*   as lightning struck our sight*
and the rain came through in torrents
*   to roots held warm in night.*